First
Facts®

MILITARY MACHINES ON DUTY

MIGHTY MILITARY AIRCRAFT

by WILLIAM N. STARK Consultant: Dennis P. Mroczkowski, Colonel, US Marine Corps (Ret.)

CAPSTONE PRESS
a capstone imprint

First Facts are published by Capstone Press,
1710 Roe Crest Drive, North Mankato, Minnesota 56003
www.mycapstone.com

Library of Congress Cataloging-in-Publication Data
Stark, William N.
 Mighty military aircraft / by William N. Stark.
  pages cm. – (First facts. Military machines on duty)
  Includes bibliographical references and index.
  Summary: "Gives readers a quick look at modern military
aircraft"– Provided by publisher.
  Audience: Grades K-3.
  ISBN 978-1-4914-8845-4 (hardcover)
  ISBN 978-1-4914-8849-2 (ebook pdf)
 1. Airplanes, Military—United States—Juvenile literature. I. Title.
 UG1243.S84 2016
 358.4'1830973—dc23
                                                    2015029638

Editorial Credits: Mandy Robbins, editor; Kristi Carlson and Katelin Plekkenpol,
designers; Jo Miller, media researcher; Gene Bentdahl, production specialist

Photo Credits: U.S. Air Force photo, 21, Capt. Shannon Collins, 9, Master Sgt.
Donald R. Allen, Cover (top), Samuel King Jr., 7, Senior Airman Carlin Leslie, 13,
Staff Sgt. Bennie J. Davis III, 15; U.S. Army photo by Spc. Glenn M. Anderson,
USAREUR Public Affairs, 17; U.S. Marine Corps photo by Cpl. Unique B. Roberts,
Cover (bottom), 5; U.S. Navy Photo by MCSN Zhiwei Tan, 1, PO1 Jonathan
Carmichael, 11, courtesy of Northrop Grumman, 19

Design Element: Shutterstock: Grebnev (metal texture background)

Printed in the United States of America in North Mankato, Minnesota
092015   009221CGS16

TABLE OF CONTENTS

Flying into the Future 4

F-15 Eagle 6

F-16 Fighting Falcon 8

CV-22 Osprey. 10

B-52 Stratofortress. 12

B-2 Spirit. 14

UH-60 Black Hawk 16

Bell Fire-X 18

Amazing but True! 20

Glossary 22

Read More 23

Internet Sites .23

Critical Thinking Using
the Common Core 23

Index 24

FLYING INTO THE FUTURE

Modern military aircraft show exciting advances in technology. Today's aircraft can travel faster than the speed of sound. They let officers inspect faraway lands without a pilot in the **cockpit**. These machines are designed to keep people as safe as possible. The military uses them in times of **combat** and of peace.

cockpit—the area in the front of a plane where the pilot sits

combat—fighting between militaries

F-15 EAGLE

Like real eagles, the F-15 Eagle fighter plane soars through the sky with power. This twin-**turbo** engine plane has excellent control in even the worst weather. Inside the cockpit, **radar** marks other planes as "friend" or "foe." As of 2015 the F-15 Eagle had a perfect combat record. It has been used in both Iraq and Afghanistan.

turbo—a type of engine that has high-pressure air forced into its cylinders by a turbine, producing extra power

radar—a device that uses radio waves to track the location of objects

F-16 FIGHTING FALCON

This single-engine plane has a "bubble" cockpit window. Good **visibility** makes the F-16 a fine daytime flyer. It speeds up to 1,620 miles (2,607 kilometers) per hour. The F-16 was the first military aircraft with a Global Positioning System (GPS). GPS tells pilots where they are at all times.

FACT:

The F-16 is the most popular fighter plane in the world. Besides the United States, countries such as Israel, Pakistan, Greece, and Turkey use the F-16 too.

visibility—how well one's surroundings can be seen clearly

CV-22 OSPREY

The CV-22 Osprey is a cross between a helicopter and a plane. Two tilting **rotors** help it take off and land **vertically**. Four crew members fit inside. It can carry 10,000 pounds (4,536 kilograms) of **cargo**. The U.S. Marines and Air Force have used the Osprey in Iraq and Afghanistan.

rotor—a set of rotating blades that lifts an aircraft off the ground

vertical—straight up and down

cargo—the goods carried by a ship, vehicle, or aircraft

B-52 STRATOFORTRESS

The Air Force has used the B-52 Stratofortress bomber since the 1950s. In its early days, it was known for speed. More recently B-52s have been used for spy work. They can also support ground troops in battle. A B-52 can drop bombs from 50,000 feet (15,240 meters) in the air.

B-2 SPIRIT

The public first saw the B-2 Spirit in 1988. The development of this flying wing aircraft had been top secret. This bomber can dodge enemy radar. Its wing design makes the Spirit hard to spot. But the aircraft's design also makes it tricky to control. Its two-person crew are among the Air Force's best pilots.

UH-60 BLACK HAWK

Nations all over the world use **variations** of the American Black Hawk utility helicopter (UH). The U.S. Army uses it to move supplies and troops during war. It also brings aid to people hurt by natural disasters. Many Black Hawks have special features. Some have medical equipment used to treat wounded people.

FACT:

The UH-60 Black Hawk can carry a total of 11,620 pounds (5,271 kg) of cargo.

variation—something that is slightly different from another thing of the same type

BELL FIRE-X

The Bell Fire-X is an **unmanned** aerial vehicle (UAV). Its top rotor has four blades and its tail rotor has two. This UAV can stay in the air for 24 hours. It can carry up to 1,000 pounds (454 kg) of cargo. The Bell Fire-X resupplies U.S. Navy ships at sea. Taking off and landing vertically helps it land in small spaces.

FACT:

People developed the first UAVs in the early 1900s during World War I (1914–1918). The war ended before they could be put to use.

unmanned—describes a vehicle that carries no people and is controlled from the ground

AMAZING BUT TRUE!

In 1942 the U.S. military needed more pilots. Most men were fighting in World War II (1939–1945). For the first time, women were invited to fly for the Air Force. More than 1,000 women trained to become members of the Women's Airforce Service Pilots (WASP). These women were not actual members of the military. They did work that freed up male pilots for combat.

GLOSSARY

cargo *(KAR-goh)*—the goods carried by a ship, vehicle, or aircraft

cockpit *(KOK-pit)*—the area in the front of a plane where the pilot sits

combat *(KOM-bat)*—fighting between militaries

radar *(RAY-dar)*—a device that uses radio waves to track the location of objects

rotor *(ROH-tur)*—a set of rotating blades that lifts an aircraft off the ground

turbo *(TUR-boh)*—a type of engine that has high-pressure air forced into its cylinders by a turbine, producing extra power

unmanned *(UHN-mand)*—describes a vehicle that carries no people and is controlled from the ground

variation *(vair-ee-AY-shuhn)*—something that is slightly different from another thing of the same type

vertical *(VUR-tuh-kuhl)*—straight up and down

visibility *(viz-uh-BIL-uh-tee)*—how well one's surroundings can be seen clearly

READ MORE

Aboff, Marcie. *The World's Fastest Machines*. Extreme Machines. Chicago: Raintree, 2011.

Alpert, Barbara. *U.S. Military Fighter Planes*. U.S. Military Technology. North Mankato, Minn.: Capstone, 2013.

Hamilton, John. *UH-60 Black Hawk*. Xtreme Military Aircraft. Minneapolis: ABDO Pub. Co., 2013.

INTERNET SITES

FactHound offers a safe, fun way to find Internet sites related to this book. All of the sites on FactHound have been researched by our staff.

Here's all you do:

Visit **www.facthound.com**

Type in this code: 9781491488454

Super-cool stuff!

Check out projects, games and lots more at
www.capstonekids.com

CRITICAL THINKING USING THE COMMON CORE

1. Why do you think women were not allowed to serve as actual members of the military? (Integration of Knowledge and Ideas)

2. What types of missions would a helicopter be more useful for than an airplane? (Key Ideas and Details)

INDEX

Afghanistan, 6, 10, 13

bombers, 12, 14
  B-2 Spirit, 14, 15
  B-52 Stratofortress, 12, 13

cargo, 10, 17, 18
cockpit, 4, 6, 8
CV-22 Osprey, 10, 11

Desert Storm, 13

fighter jets, 5, 6, 9
  F-15, 6, 7
  F-16 Fighting Falcon, 8, 9
  F-35 Lightning II, 5

Global Positioning System
  (GPS), 8

Iraq, 6, 10, 13

Mau, Christine, 5

pilots, 4, 8, 14, 20

radar, 6, 14

speed, 4, 8, 12

UAVs, 18, 19
  Bell Fire-X, 18
UH-60 Black Hawk, 16, 17
U.S. Air Force, 5, 10, 12, 14, 20
U.S. Army, 16
U.S. Marines, 10
U.S. Navy, 18

Vietnam War, 13

Women's Airforce Service
  Pilots (WASP), 20
World War I, 19
World War II, 20